The Basket Maker

Also from Westphalia Press
westphaliapress.org

The Idea of the Digital University

Bulwarks Against Poverty in America

Treasures of London

Avate Garde Politician

L'Enfant and the Freemasons

Baronial Bedrooms

Making Trouble for Muslims

Philippine Masonic Directory ~ 1918

Paddle Your Own Canoe

Opportunity and Horatio Alger

Careers in the Face of Challenge

Bookplates of the Kings

Hymns to the Gods

Freemasonry in Old Buffalo

Original Cables from the Pearl Harbor Attack

Social Satire and the Modern Novel

The Essence of Harvard

The Genius of Freemasonry

A Definitive Commentary on Bookplates

James Martineau and Rebuilding Theology

Bohemian San Francisco

The Wizard

Crime 3.0

Anti-Masonry and the Murder of Morgan

Understanding Art

Spies I Knew

Lodge "Himalayan Brotherhood" No. 459 C.E.

Ancient Masonic Mysteries

Collecting Old Books

Masonic Secret Signs and Passwords

Death Valley in '49

Lariats and Lassos

Mr. Garfield of Ohio

The Wisdom of Thomas Starr King

The French Foreign Legion

War in Syria

Naturism Comes to the United States

New Sources on Women and Freemasonry

Designing, Adapting, Strategizing in Online Education

Gunboat and Gun-runner

Memoirs of a Poor Relation

Espionage!

Bohemian San Francisco

Tales of Old Japan

The Basket Maker

by Luther Weston Turner

WESTPHALIA PRESS
An imprint of Policy Studies Organization

The Basket Maker: An Illustrated Guide to 20th Century Basket Weaving
All Rights Reserved © 2015 by Policy Studies Organization

Westphalia Press
An imprint of Policy Studies Organization
1527 New Hampshire Ave., NW
Washington, D.C. 20036
info@ipsonet.org

ISBN-13: 978-1-63391-188-8
ISBN-10: 1633911888

Cover design by Taillefer Long at Illuminated Stories:
www.illuminatedstories.com

Daniel Gutierrez-Sandoval, Executive Director
PSO and Westphalia Press

Updated material and comments on this edition
can be found at the Westphalia Press website:
www.westphaliapress.org

THE
BASKET MAKER

BY

LUTHER WESTON TURNER
DIRECTOR OF MANUAL TRAINING IN THE HILL SCHOOL
POTTSTOWN, PENNSYLVANIA

ATKINSON, MENTZER & GROVER
NEW YORK   CHICAGO   BOSTON   DALLAS

BASKETRY

Basketry has been called one of the fads of the newest education. It was one of the essentials of the oldest education. Basketry still holds a commanding position among the arts of men, even in countries called highly civilized. Its place in schools is still somewhat in dispute, but unquestionably it offers to children a clean and educative handicraft. Properly taught, it vitalizes certain periods in history, fosters motor control, develops judgment and taste, and familiarizes the pupil with one of the ancient and honorable occupations of mankind.

Mr. Turner knows his subject thoroughly, having tramped with Indians for materials, worked with Indians for processes, practised with pupils for methods, and studied with specialists for tasteful results. The chapters of this booklet appeared first as illustrated articles in The School Arts Book, beginning in April 1905. The demand for them has been so great that the supply of magazines is exhausted, and this reprint is made to meet what is evidently a wide-spread demand for first class instruction in the basic principles of this important kind of manual art.

Henry Turner Bailey

THE BASKET MAKER

I. INTRODUCTORY WORK

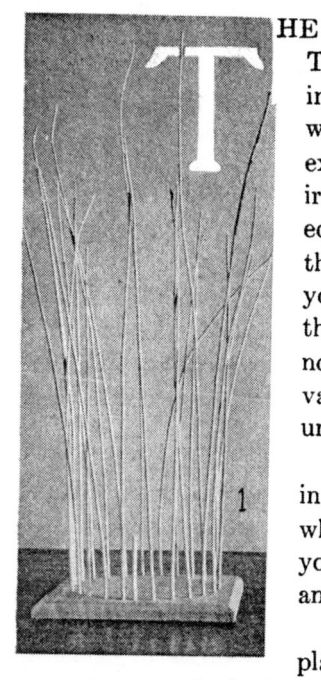

THE fruition of thought is expression. Thought along the lines of manual training is susceptible of expression in many ways and through many mediums. The expression of thought through wood and iron necessitates a more or less elaborate equipment of tools, and for this reason those mediums of expression are denied younger pupils. But the expression of thought through basketry, requires almost no tools (a knife and scratch-awl), has variety as to form and color and almost unlimited possibilities in design.

It is my aim in this booklet to give in simple English and with illustrations which may be comprehended by the youngest pupil, the results of my thought and teaching of basketry.

I believe the poor results seen in many places are due to poor teaching. Teachers are not, as a rule, insistent enough at the beginning. Good results can only be secured by close attention to basic details. A pupil should not be allowed to progress who cannot make the bottom of a basket and have it strong and closely woven. He must understand that no basket can be firmly made unless its foundation is right.

The ordinary pupil is, and should be, an animated question mark. "Why?" "What for?" and "What makes it do that?"

are the ever recurring questions. "Why do you have to have an odd number of spokes with a single weaver?" was the first question asked in the class this year.

In order to answer this and many other questions which arise, I have found it necessary to devise some means by which a verbal explanation can be demonstrated to the satisfaction of the dullest pupil. The device is a small piece of board, any size and thickness, on which a circle of any size is drawn. The circumference of this circle is divided off into spaces about ⅝ of an inch apart, and holes are bored, into which pieces of willow or reed are inserted, Fig. 1. The spacing would better not be equal, as one hole is to contain a peg which may be taken out in order to get an odd or an even number of uprights. By this device a pupil can answer his own question, and discover much about different weaves. The uprights will hereafter be known as stakes. Figure 2 shows the single weave with an odd number of stakes. Figure 3 shows the same with an even number. Figure 4 shows the Indian method of weaving with a single weaver and an even number of stakes. When the weaver gets around to where it started, it is passed behind two stakes, and the weaving is continued as before, the weaver passing behind the next two stakes on each course.

The illustrative weaving in this chapter is done in colors, in order that the course of one weaver may be followed more easily, and also to suggest from the beginning the possibilities of design and decoration by the use of a combination of plain and colored weavers.* If the essential elements of construction, (the stakes and weavers) are used as decorative features wherever possible, much of the trouble about decoration and design in basketry will be done away with.

---

*Mr. Chas. E. Mather, Braggville, Mass., has the finest variety of colors for weavers which I have as yet found. Both the aniline and vegetable colors do not run while working and they both seem to be permanent.

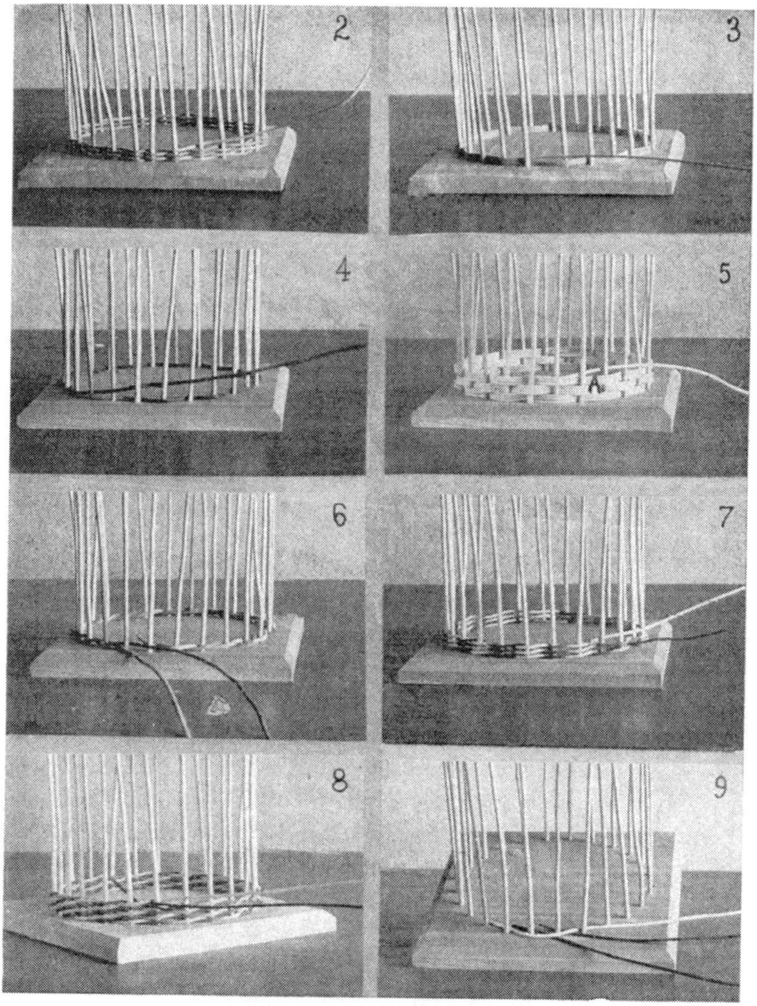
2
3
4
5
6
7
8
9

Figure 5 shows a decorative feature made possible by the use of a single weaver and an even number of stakes. At A may be seen the method of changing from one course to another. Either two, three, or four rows may be woven before changing courses, and as many courses may be woven as the design of the basket may require. This of course is left to the judgment of the pupil or teacher.

Figure 6 shows the double or pairing weave (*i. e.* weaving with two weavers) and Figure 7 suggests the possibilities in decoration, when one weaver is colored and an even number of stakes are used.

Figure 8 shows the design when the pairing weave is used with an odd number of spokes and also the method of joining weaves in either double, triple or quadruple weaving. The end of the new weaver is inserted behind and beside the end of the one already woven in, and the weaving continues as if the weavers were continuous. The end of the old weaver can then be cut off flush with the outside of the basket, and the end of the new one flush with the inside.

In weaving with two, three, or four weavers the left hand one of the group is always known as the rear weaver and the right hand one as the forward weaver, and weaving is always done from left to right except in cases of special design. Such cases will be spoken of in a later chapter.

Figure 9 shows the starting of the triple weave. Three weavers are put behind three consecutive stakes and project toward the right. The rear one goes over the other two and in front of two stakes, behind one stake, and out between the next pair of stakes to the right of the forward weaver. The one that was the middle weaver now becomes the rear one, and it in turn is treated as the other rear one was. This process is continued as long as triple weaving is needed. Always be sure to take the rear weaver and have it come out between the pair of stakes to the right of the forward weaver.

Decorative features of triple weaving follow: Figure 10 shows the result when one colored weaver and two natural ones are used and the number of weavers (3) is equally divisible into the number of stakes. Each color forms in a vertical stripe. Using two colored and one natural weaver gives the same result but with a different proportion of color.

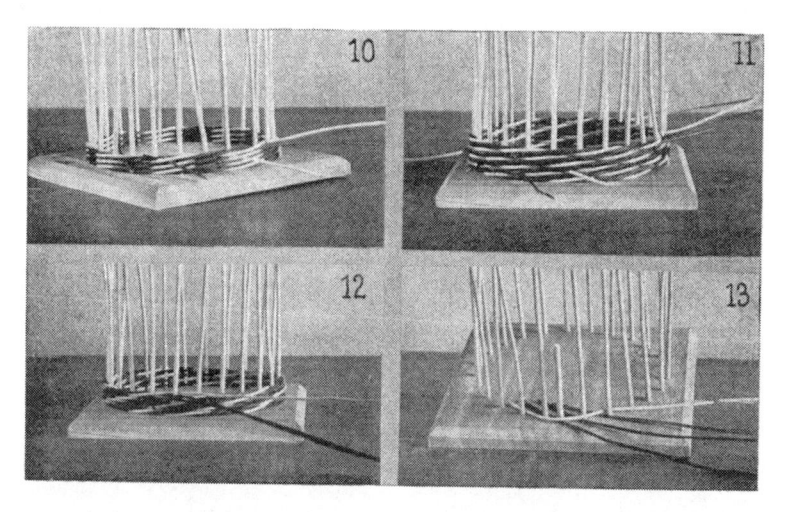

Figure 11 shows the result when the number of stakes is divisible by the number of weavers with a remainder of one. This gives the variegated effect outside and the spiral effect inside.

● Figure 12 shows the result when the number of stakes is divisible by the number of weavers with a remainder of two. This gives the variegated effect inside and the spiral effect outside.

Figure 13 shows the starting of the quadruple weave. With the decorative features already shown in other weaves, each student can find out for himself the possibilities of this weave by varying

Fig. 14.

the ratio of the stakes to the weavers and by using either one, two, or three colored weavers.

In the next chapter I will give a detailed description of the construction of several mats which embody some of the ideas here presented, and shown in the group picture, Fig. 14.

II. WEAVING FOUNDATIONS

THE one great aim of manual training is to combine judgment, a purely mental function, and execution, a purely physical one. There seems to be no work so efficient in combining the two from the beginning as basketry. The material varies so in texture that care and judgment are required in its manipulation, and so few tools are used that the hand must do all or a greater part of the work.

In all teaching the "character of work" should be emphasized rather than the intrinsic value of that which is produced by work. The aim should be to have work complete in all its parts, relatively perfect* as to beauty of design and workmanship, and finished, in so far as the completed work coming from the pupil can show his intention and evince careful and diligent work.

In manual training work the procedure should be from the simple to the complex. The teacher should never hurry the different stages of the work faster than the young mind can go. The pupil must comprehend each step. Let the motto be "Not How much, but How well."

In order to make use of the features of weaving spoken of in the first chapter it will be necessary to have a simple problem on

---

*I say "relatively perfect" feeling that while there is nothing absolutely perfect possible to the hand of man, the term may be used relatively for whatever makes the nearest approach to perfection.

which to work. Mats of various sizes are useful, may be made beautiful, and as they embody all the constructive features found in the bottom of a basket, may well be taken as the first problem.

The foundation pieces on which the weaving of a mat or the bottom of a basket is done are known as spokes because during the

weaving, they radiate from a common center like the spokes of a wheel.

A finished mat of the simplest construction is shown in Figure 1, A. For this we use an odd number of spokes and a single weaver. The material required is as follows: Four pieces of No. 3 reed 12 inches long, one piece 7 inches long and a weaver of No. 2 reed. These are held together in the left hand and grouped as shown in Figure 2.

The short odd one is between the upper end of the two vertical ones and the horizontal pair is behind the vertical group. This brings the three vertical spokes above, and in front of the horizontal pair. The weaver of No. 2 reed is placed as shown, Figure 2, behind the vertical group and along the top of the horizontal pair with its right hand end projecting about ¾ of an inch to the right of the vertical group.

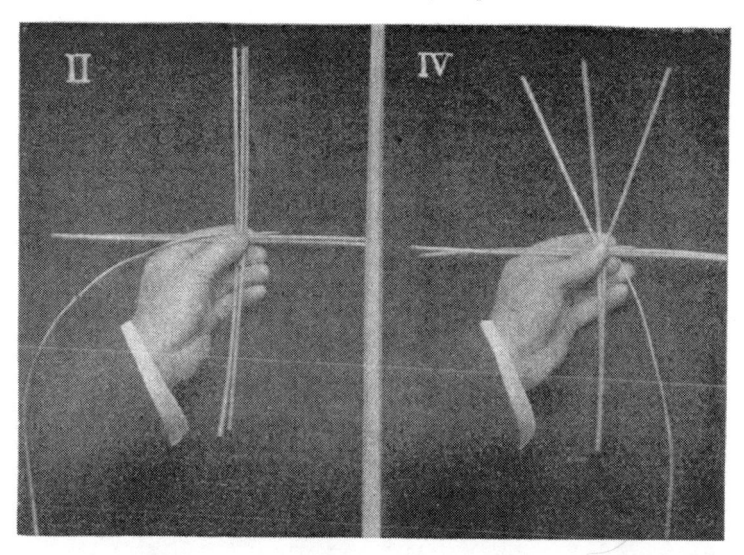

The weaver is then brought to the right in front of the vertical group, back and down behind the horizontal group, thereby binding its own end to the spokes. (Figure 3, A, shows the exact position of the weaver at this stage.)

It next comes to the left in front of the vertical and below the horizontal group, and up behind the horizontal group to the position from which it first started. It now follows the same course once more until it has been around the group twice as shown in Figure 3, B; but the next time instead of coming down across the horizontal spokes as shown in that figure, the spokes are separated and the under and over weaving commences as seen in Figure 4.

The left hand does the holding and the right hand the weaving. Be sure to hold the spokes out straight as the weaving is done around them in order that the weaver may be made to conform

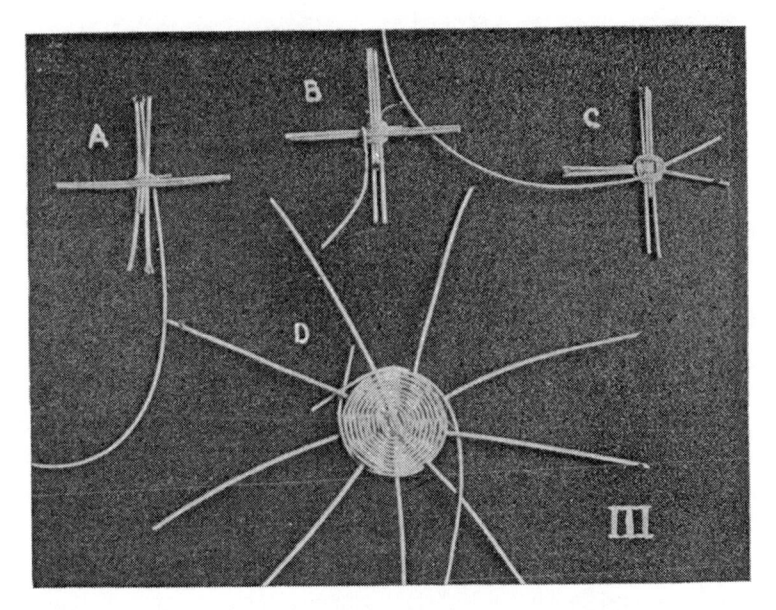

to the spokes, and not the spokes to the weaver as shown in Figure 5, A. Figure 5, B, shows the correct method. The spokes are approximately in the same horizontal plane.

When the spokes are all the same distance apart at the weaving, hold the mat down on a flat surface, Fig. 6, and continue the weaving until it is 3 inches in diameter. Figure 6 illustrates the correct position of the hands when holding the work down on a surface. Hold the spokes down with the left hand and weave with the right. This figure illustrates the weaving of a much larger mat but the principle is exactly the same. If one weaver is too short to bring the weaving to the desired size, join the weavers as shown in Figure 3, D, and continue the weaving as though the weaver were continuous, being careful to keep the weaving close together with the left hand each time it goes over and under a spoke.

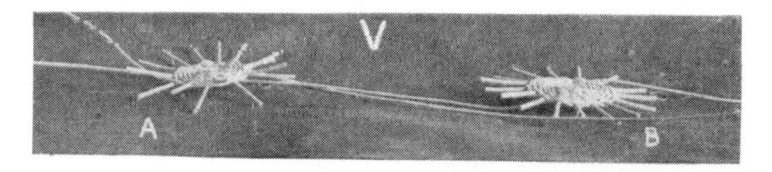

Right at this point insist upon the pupils' going slowly and weaving closely. The later satisfaction of knowing how to weave correctly will more than offset any discouragement at not seeming able to produce great results at once.

Next cut off the weaver long enough to go a little more than once around the circumference and overcast the weaving in the following manner: As the weaver comes from behind a spoke, put it over the next spoke to the right and through the last row of weaving just before it gets to the following spoke. It then goes behind that spoke, over the next and through the weaving, as before, just before it gets to the next spoke.

Figure 7 shows one stitch of overcasting and the second stitch just ready to be pulled through. This process continues once around, when the weaver is cut off on the back side of the last spoke as shown in Figure 1, B. Finish the mat with an open border, Figure 8. A, by turning in the ends of the spokes.

Figure 8 shows another "device" to illustrate the construction of some simple open borders. These may be woven left-handed or right-handed as is most convenient. In "A" one spoke goes in front of the next and inserts just before it gets to the third. In "B" one goes in front of two and inserts just before it gets to the fourth. In "C" one goes in front of three and inserts just before it gets to the fifth. In "D," in front of four and just before the sixth. Judgment is required to get the right sized loop. The length of spoke required after overcasting can be found by trial. All spokes must be cut the same length, sharpened, and inserted equally. In these borders if the spokes are approximately an inch apart "A" will require about 2¾ inches outside of the overcasting, "B" about 4¼ inches, "C" 5½ to 6½ inches, and "D" 6½ to 8½ inches. These lengths allow for insertion.

In Figure 3, A, B, and C illustrate another method of starting a center with one weaver. In this case two pieces are split in the center and the other two are put through them with the odd one inserted as shown at A. The weaving proceeds as by the first method until two courses are woven when, instead of separating the three spokes and beginning the single weaving, the weaver is reversed as shown at B and two courses are woven the other way. The separation into singles then begins as at C. This method

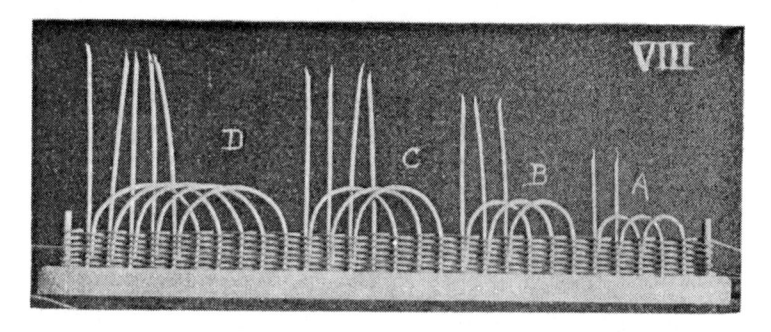

of splitting half of the spokes and putting the others through them is the better method of the two as it is the less difficult to hold the group while the first two rows are woven.

Figure 1, B, shows a mat the center of which was started by the second method. The spokes are of No. 4 reed and the weavers of No. 3. Four spokes are 12½ inches long and one, 7½ inches. The border is illustrated at A, Figure 8. The weaving was 3¼ inches in diameter before overcasting.

Figure 9 shows the method of starting a center with the pairing weave. At A three pieces pass through two pieces giving ten spokes. At B three going through three give twelve spokes. The split pieces are held horizontally, and the weaver, doubled in the middle, is started around the vertical group above the horizontal ones as shown at A; one end being in front of the other behind the vertical group, thus forming the two weavers. The front weaver then comes to the right across the vertical group, and down behind the horizontal group. The rear one goes to the right across the back of the vertical group and down in front of the horizontal group. (B shows the weaving at this stage.) The whole group of spokes is now revolved from right to left until the horizontal group becomes vertical, C, and the weaving proceeds as before, holding the work with the left hand, weaving with the right, and revolving so that a vertical group is woven over each time. Notice that the revolution is from right to left and weaving from left to right. In the illustrated weaving, spokes of No. 4 reed are used and a weaver of No. 2 reed.*

When three pieces cross three pieces it is necessary to go around the groups three times before separating into singles, Fig. 9, D. As soon as it is possible after separating, get the spokes the same distance apart at the weaving. If they are spread apart as at E, this can be done in two courses and single weaving can be commenced. Take the rear weaver and bring it over one spoke and under the next, and so on once around until coming to the other weaver. F shows it at this stage. Notice that when a course is woven once around, the weaver comes outside of the other weaver and stops. The inside one now weaves around until it comes to the same position, with reference to the first one, that the first one held to it. Continue to weave first one and then the other, each as in single weaving, until the desired diameter is reached. Overcast as shown in Figure 10. The weavers are stopped on opposite sides of the weaving, A, and the top one is overcast to the other, B. The lower one is then overcast until

---

*It is wise to have the reed for the spokes and stakes two sizes larger than the weaver except in cases where the bottom is less than three inches in diameter, when a difference of one size is sufficient.

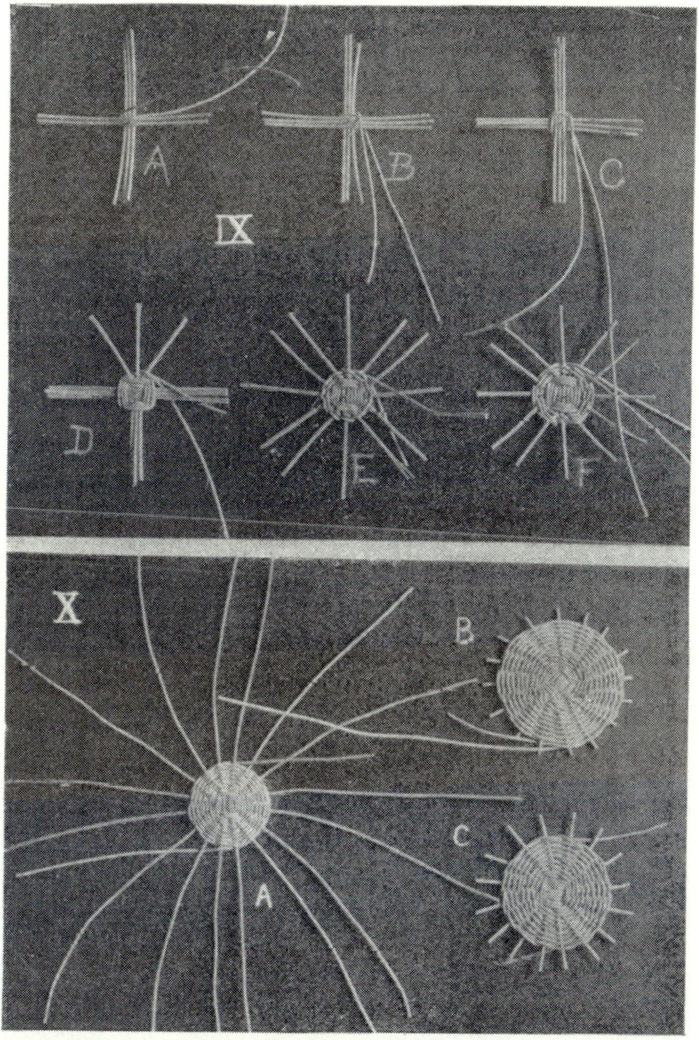
A
B
C
IX
D
E
F
X
B
A
C

it comes opposite to where the other overcasting stopped, C. Weavers can then be cut off on the back side of the weaving. If the bottom of the basket is to be woven, it must be crowned slightly, and the weaving may be done over the knee, as shown in Figure 11. (See initial.) This figure also shows the correct method of holding the hands when weaving either a bottom or a small mat.

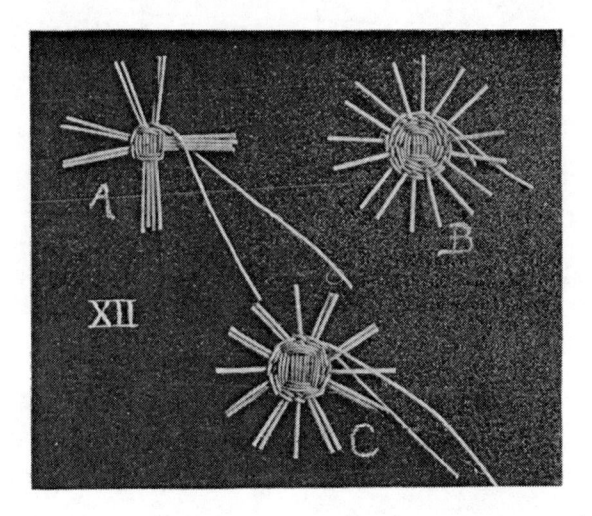

Figure 12 shows the method of starting a sixteen spoke center. Four pieces cross four pieces, and two rows of pairing are woven around the groups of fours before they are separated into twos, A. Two rows are then woven around the pairs before separating them into singles, B. When the desired diameter is woven, overcast as shown in Figure 10.

Figure 12, C, shows the method of weaving a center having 20 spokes. Here five cross five. Three rows of pairing are woven around the groups of fives and then a pair is separated from each side of the center one of each group, forming eight pairs and four single spokes. These are woven around twice and then separated into singles. C shows the work just before the separation into singles.

The large mat, Fig. 1, C, with open border is made as follows: Cut 10 pieces of No. 5 reed 23 inches long. Split five in the center and put five through them. Weave center $2\frac{1}{2}$ inches in diameter, as described in Figure 12, C, with a No. 2 weaver. Cut off the weavers on opposite sides, Fig. 10, A, and start with 2 No. 3 weavers, weaving until the work is $4\frac{1}{2}$ inches in diameter. Notice in Figure 6 how the left hand holds the work down to the surface and the right hand does the weaving. When the weaving is $4\frac{1}{2}$ inches in diameter stop the weaving as before and insert two colored weavers, weaving four rows, two on each side of the spokes. Then start the natural weavers again and weave until the weaving is seven inches in diameter. Overcast as shown in Figure 10 and finish the edge as in C, Fig. 8. Spokes want to be about $7\frac{3}{4}$ inches long outside of the overcasting and must be sharpened on the end and inserted about $1\frac{3}{4}$ inches into the weaving.

Whenever the word "about" is used the subject requires the personal judgment of the one doing the work. If there is any difference in the texture of the reeds, always select the hardest ones for the spokes and use the softest ones for weaving.

III. MATS

THIS chapter contains all that will be said, in this booklet, about mats. But let me say,--"Not half has been told" of the designs which might be woven into mats and basket covers. Read over the first chapters on weaving and then see how many designs can be thought out by one who does some thinking for himself.

Figure 1 shows six mats. A and B are the same diameter, of equally good workmanship, and are woven with the same kind of weaving. So are C and D. To be critical, A lacks color. It is supplied in B. The spirals in C seem to be "in the air," neither starting from anything nor ending anywhere. In D this is overcome by starting them from a band of color and having them die into a similar band, thus giving unity to the whole design. Woven bands in poor proportion are worse than plain weaving. Just enough color must be added in the right place to give proper tone and balance.

Figure 2 shows another device for illustrating work. This gives the construction of closed borders. The four illustrated are the simplest which can be made. In weaving them around the edge of a mat the weaving is started either at the top or right-hand side and continued around in the direction of the movement of the hands of a clock. When using these borders on a basket the weaving is started on the side nearest to you and continues from left to right, while the basket itself is moved from right to left. In A and B the left hand figure shows the starting of the first row of the weaving and the right hand figure the finished row.

Let us suppose the left hand spoke in each case is No. 1 and that the others follow to the right in order. In A, No. 1 goes behind No. 2 and out; No. 2 behind No. 3 and out; and so on around the circumference, the last spoke going behind No. 1 and out of

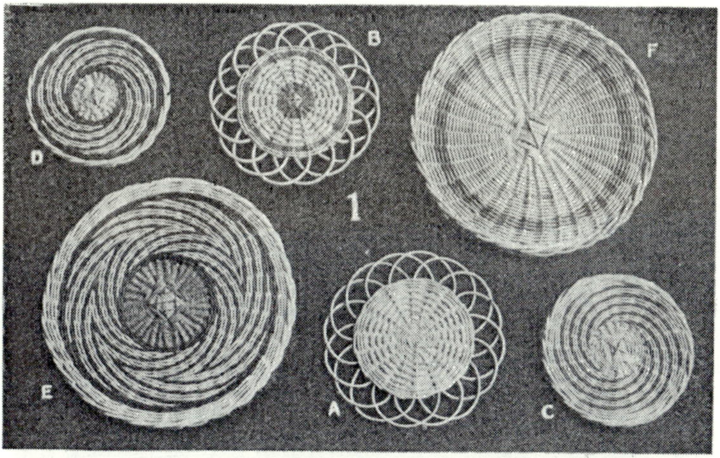
1
A
B
C
D
E
F

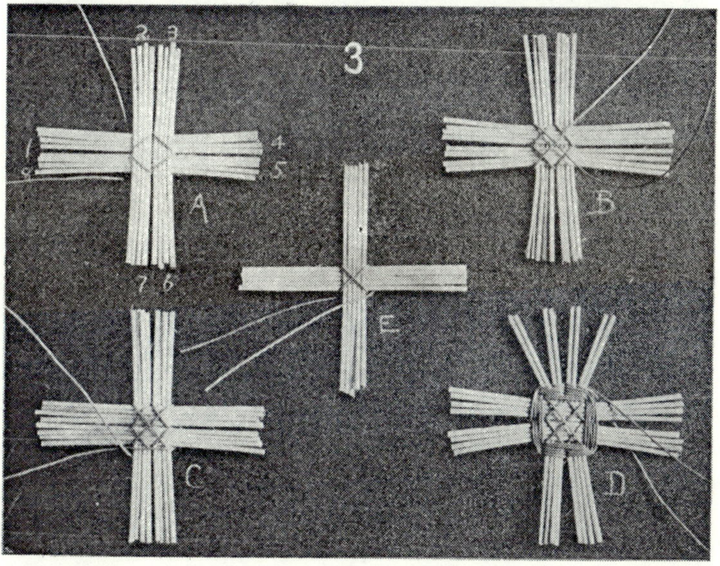
3
1
2 3
4
5
6
7
8
A
B
C
D
E

the loop left by it in going behind No. 2. Pull all ends tightly to the right, finishing the first row as at A, (left). For the second row, start with any spoke, put it in front of the next to the right and through the loop, into the inside of the basket just before getting to the next spoke. A (right) shows a portion of the finished border. The ends of the spokes are next cut off just inside of the border and close to it. In B, in the first row each spoke goes to the

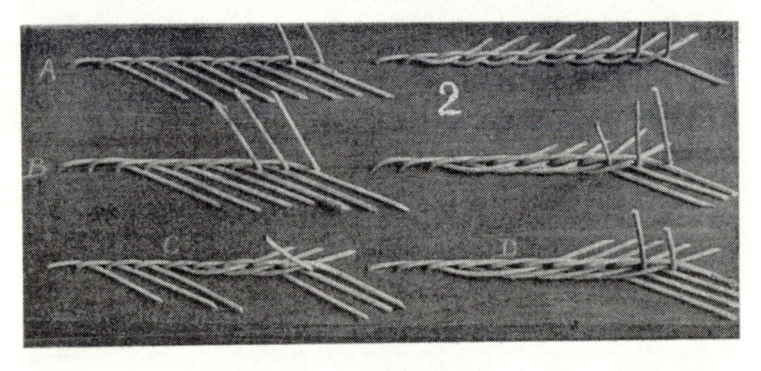

right behind two and out. In the next row in front of two and through to the inside just before getting to the next. In the first row of C, each goes behind one and out and in the second row, in front of two and to the inside. In D, each goes behind two and out in the first row, and in front of three and in, in the second row. If the spokes are approximately one inch apart A will take 3½ inches outside of overcasting, B 5½ inches, C 4½ inches, and D 6½ inches.

Mat B, Fig. 1, is made as follows: For material—Eight pieces of No. 5 rattan 17½ inches long and some No. 2 natural and colored weavers. Split four of the No. 5 pieces and put the other four through them.

The center is started with a colored weaver, as shown at E, Fig. 3. Double the weaver near its center and put the loop back of the horizontal group and to the left of the vertical group, having one weaver come to the front above the horizontal group and the other to the front below it. Bring the lower one to the right and up diagonally across the vertical group, and then down behind the horizontal group and to the front. Then bring the upper one to the right, diagonally across the vertical group, and to the left behind the vertical group below the horizontal. This will bring the weavers in the exact position shown in the cut. The whole thing may now be revolved until the weavers come above the horizontal group, and the weaving may progress according to the directions for a sixteen spoke center (Figure 12, previous chapter). When the spokes are evenly separated into singles the weaving should be about 1½ inches in diameter.

Cut off the weavers on the back side and start a natural weaver as shown in Figure 4. Weave with this until the work is about four inches in diameter, using the decorative feature spoken of in chapter I, Fig. 5, Indian method. Figure 5 shows the weaver passing behind two spokes in order that it may start on the second row of double weaving.

Figure 6 shows the stopping of this weaving and the starting of the band of color. Weave five or six rows of the color and then two rows of natural weaving. Instead of overcasting all around as described in the previous chapter, the weaver may be stopped by tucking it through the last row of weaving once, as shown at A, Fig. 7. In Figure 7 notice also the single spiral made by the consecutive crossing of two spokes by the weaver as the weaving changes from one course to the next. This is a result of the Indian method of working one weaver with an even number of spokes. If the above single overcast of one stitch does not seem satisfactory, overcast the edge of the mat as shown in Figure 7, chapter II.

Mark off the spokes with a pencil 4½ inches from the overcasting and finish with open border, B, Fig. 8, chapter II, inserting

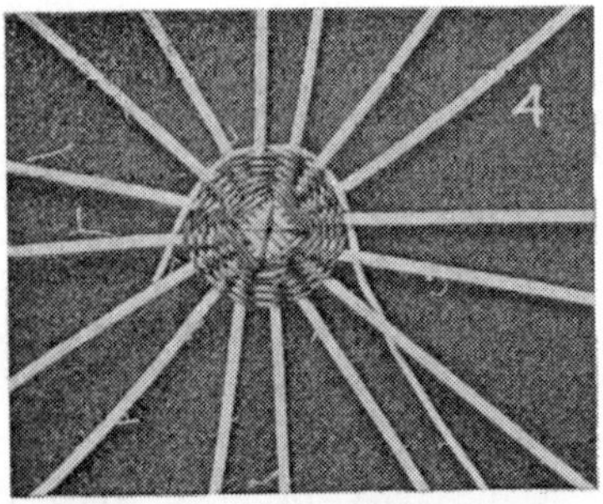
4

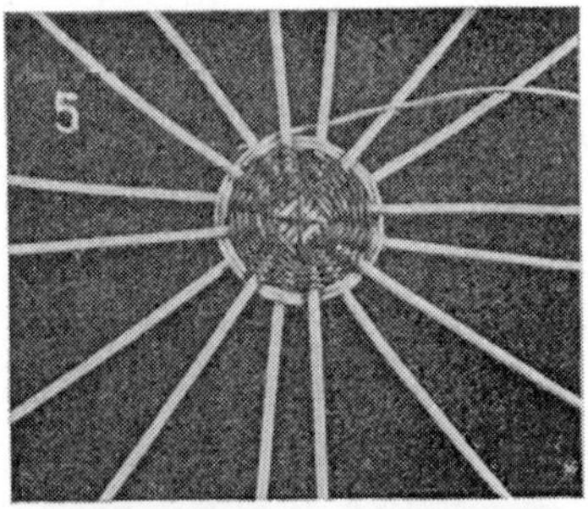
5

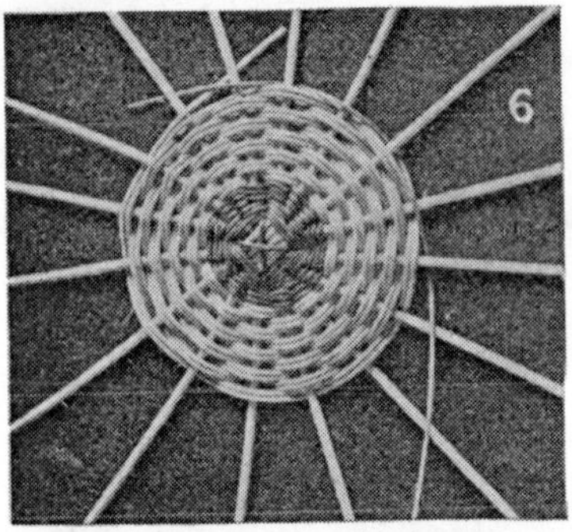
6

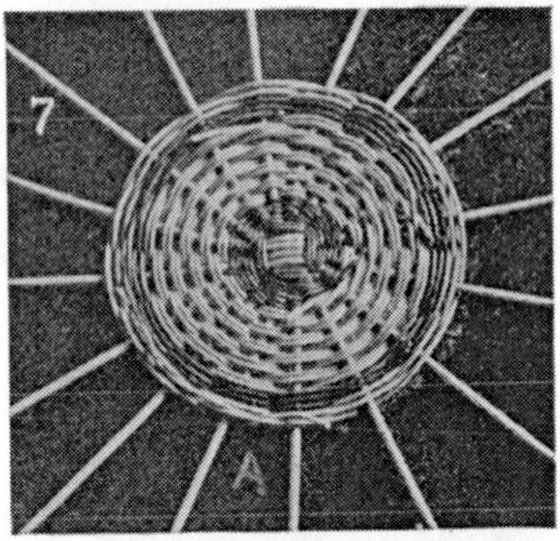
7
A

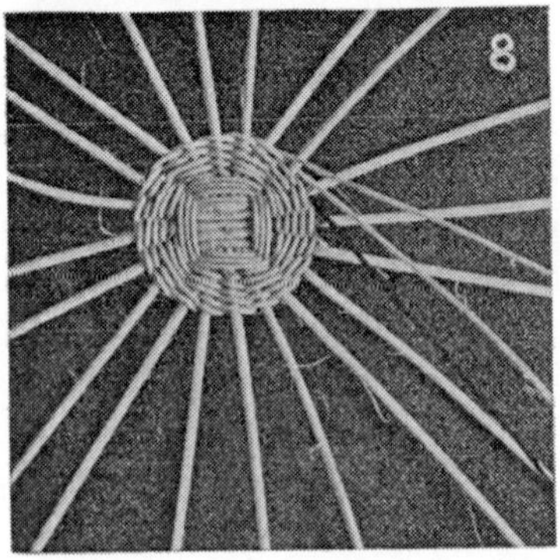
8

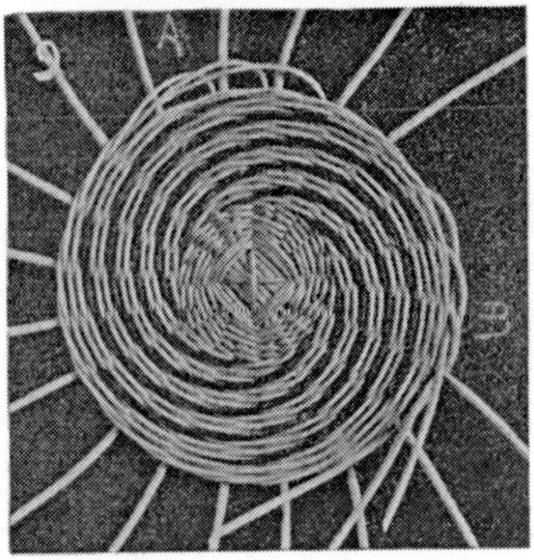
9
A
B

each spoke to the mark. In this way the loops of the border can be made the same size.

For mat C, five spokes of No. 5 reed 17½ inches long pass through five similar spokes. A No. 3 natural weaver is started either as shown in Figure 3, or in Figure 9, chapter II, and woven until the spokes are evenly separated into singles. The weaving will then be about 2½ inches in diameter. Lay the work on a flat surface, bring both weavers above the spokes and insert a colored weaver between the next two spokes to the right, as shown in Figure 8. Weave with the triple weave until about 5¾ inches in diameter. Cut the colored weaver out and insert a natural one in its place. Weave two courses of natural weaving and stop the weavers, as shown in Figure 9, A. Push them down close to the other weaving. (These are left up in the illustration simply to show the method of insertion beside the stakes.)

With the mat still down on a surface, commence to bind off the edge, Fig. 9, B, using close border, B, Fig. 2. The last two spokes are put through the loops left by starting the first two, Fig. 9, as shown in Figure 10. All are pulled tightly to the right, the second row is woven, pulled tightly, and the spokes cut off on the back side close to the border.

Figure 11 shows the under side before the spokes are cut off. Notice the difference in the effect of the weaving on the two sides and reflect upon it. You may want just that effect sometime as a decorative feature. Learn to take advantage of things that only seem to "happen so."

Mat D is started the same as mat C and woven with the same stitch. Two rows of colored weaving are woven before starting the spirals, and two rows after the spirals are the desired size. The border may be any of the closed borders in Figure 2.

Mat E is made with the thirty-two spoke center, illustrated in Figure 3. The following material is required: Sixteen spokes of No. 6 natural reed 24 inches long and weavers of Nos. 2 and 3 reed. The weavers are of three tones, light (natural), dark (colored), and a middle value (colored). Eight spokes are put through eight spokes, as shown at A, Figure 3. A No. 2 weaver of the neutral shade is bent in the middle and the pairing weave is started, as follows: The loop of the weaver is put through the spokes between groups 1-8, Fig. 3, A, and the pairing weave goes diagonally around

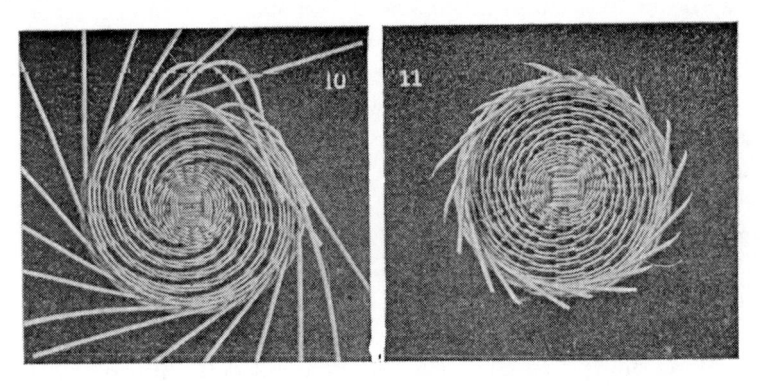

from 1-8 to 2-3, 4-5, 6-7, and from between 6-7 one weaver goes across the back of 2-7 and out to the left below the horizontal group, as shown, and the other goes diagonally across the face of 2-7, between 1-8 and up behind group 1, as shown.

The weavers next go through stages B and C as follows: The upper one is brought diagonally down across the horizontal group of eight and to the left behind the vertical group; the lower one diagonally up, across the face of the vertical group of eight, then down behind the horizontal group and to the left across the face of the vertical group to the position shown at C. The pairing weave now commences around the groups of eight until two rows have been woven, when they separate into groups of fours, and the weaving continues three times around before separating into pairs.

It will be found necessary to weave around the pairs four or five times before separating into singles. D shows the separation into fours and the beginning of the separation into pairs. The singles should be sufficiently far apart after five or six rows have been woven around them to allow the triple weaving to be commenced.

Up to this stage the weaving is all done in the hands, and great care must be taken to keep it close together. Every time the weaver is put between two spokes, from the front to the back side, it must be pulled down with the right hand on to the weaving already done, as shown in Figure 12, holding the "tension" thus gained with the middle finger of the left hand until the other weaver is brought across it to the front between the same pair of spokes. The weaver which has just been brought to the front must now be pulled down, as shown in Figure 13. The tension is still held with the middle finger of the left hand until the weaver, shown in Figure 13, is put back between the next pair of spokes to the right.

If a little care is given to this matter of "tension" the weaving can be very closely done. Cut off the No. 2 weaver on the back side and take three dark No. 3 weavers and insert, as shown in Figure 14, holding the ends of the weavers with the left hand until two or three stitches are taken. (This Figure shows natural weavers, in order to more clearly illustrate the starting of the triple weave.) The work is now held down on a flat surface, as shown in Figure 15. Weave two rows of dark and then cut out two of the dark weavers and insert natural ones in their places, weaving eight rows of triple weaving. Cut off all three weavers and start the weaving the other way, inserting the new weavers, as shown in Figure 16. These push down into the weaving, to the right of and beside the spokes, and are brought behind the spokes and out where the others stopped. Do not get the colors mixed. Weave eight rows the other way and then cut the two natural ones out,

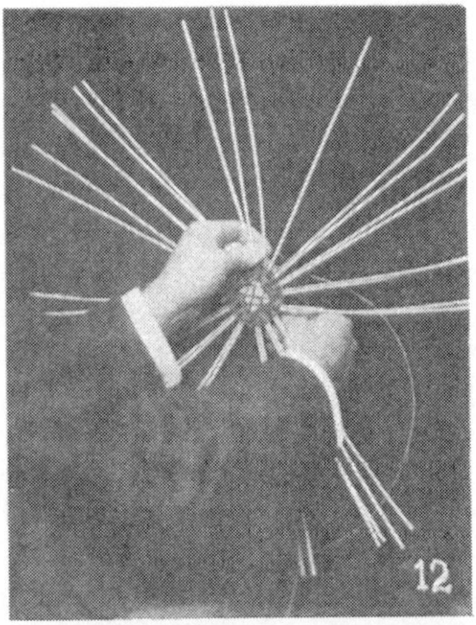
12

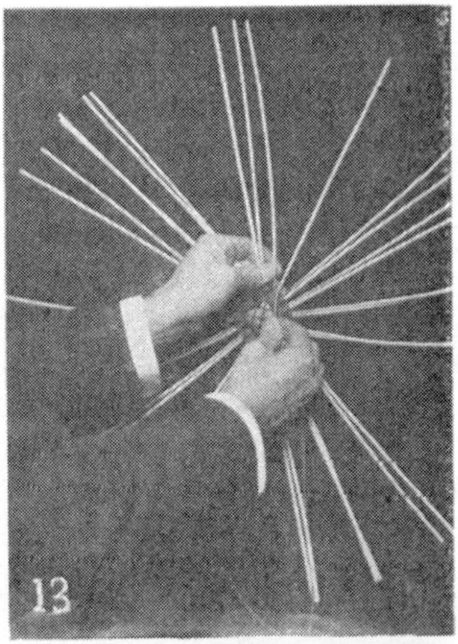
13

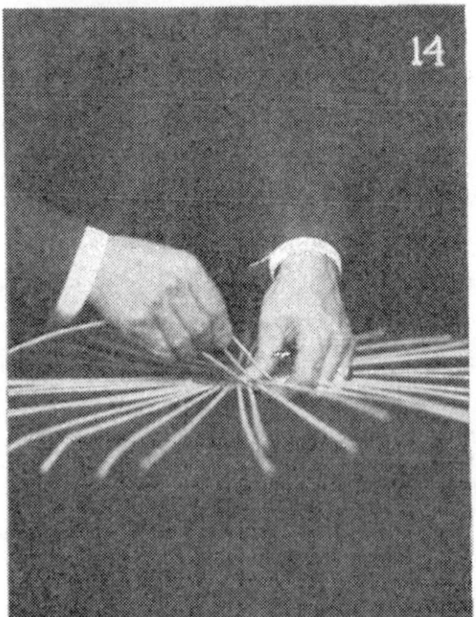
14

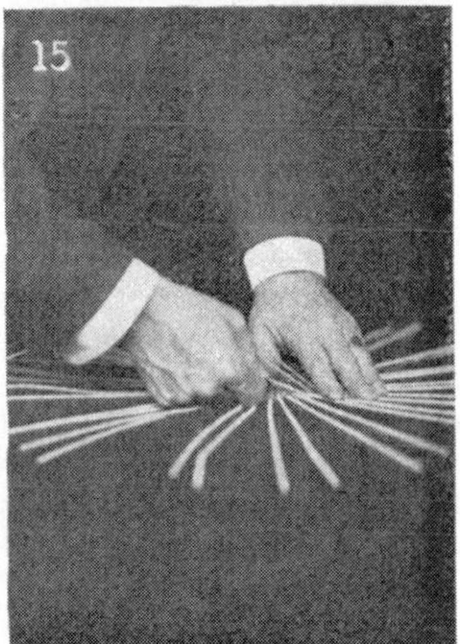
15

inserting two dark ones in their places, and weaving two rows to form the outer band. Cut off all three weavers and insert the ends as shown in Figure 9, A. Then start three natural weavers and weave the three outer rows to form the outer band of natural color. Start these as in Figure 16 and end them as in Figure 9, A.

Figure 17 shows the mat, about eleven inches in diameter, ready to close the border. Use border C, Fig. 2, starting at the top. This design may be known as the "Indian arrow head" design.

By finishing the edge of mat C, Fig. 1, illustrated in the previous chapter, a mat similar to F, Fig. 1, of this chapter would be the result.

The design is shown on a basket illustrated in Figure 14, chapter I, at A.

At B, Figure 14, chapter I, the same ideas carried further give the "Lightning Flash" design.

IV. THE SIMPLEST BASKET

THE first small basket is but little more difficult to make than the first mat. The spokes are a little longer to allow for turning up, and are of the same sized reed.

Figure 1 shows the successive steps in the construction of the simplest basket. The weaving is started as in Figure 2, chapter II, and is continued until it is about $1\frac{7}{8}$ inches in diameter, when the spokes are turned up and become stakes. A glance at Figure 1, a, will show why all the stakes do not stay in a perpendicular position the first time the weaver goes around them. Figure 1, b, shows the weaver twice around and the stakes all standing erect.

The future shape of the basket is determined at this point in the weaving. If a straight, perpendicular-sided basket is wanted, Fig. 1, e, give the weaver tension enough to hold the stakes upright after three or four rows of weaving. If a straight, flaring-sided basket is wanted, Figure 2, a, do not give the first rows of weaving so much tension, thereby allowing the stakes to flare. In weaving all straight-sided baskets, after the stakes stand at a satisfactory angle, be very careful to see that the weaver has no tension whatever. Personal taste and good judgment are the factors which determine the angle of the flare. If a curved-sided basket is wanted, Fig. 2, b, start with the stakes quite flaring, and keep an even tension on the weaver as the weaving progresses and until the desired curve is woven in. Always remember that tension on the weaver will bring the stakes together. Figure 3 shows the correct method of holding a small basket during the weaving of the sides.

When the basket is woven to the desired height, overcast the weaving around the stakes just as it was done around the spokes of the mat. This process was described and illustrated in chapter II, Fig. 7. The basket may then be finished satisfactorily by using either border, a or b, chapter II, Fig. 8. Make the stakes long enough to push through the weaving, as shown in Figure 1, d. This will stiffen the sides of the basket, and give it a more finished appearance. After all the stakes are pushed through, get the curves and loops of the border all regular in outline and the same height either by measurement or by turning the basket bottom side up on a flat surface and making all the loops touch the surface.

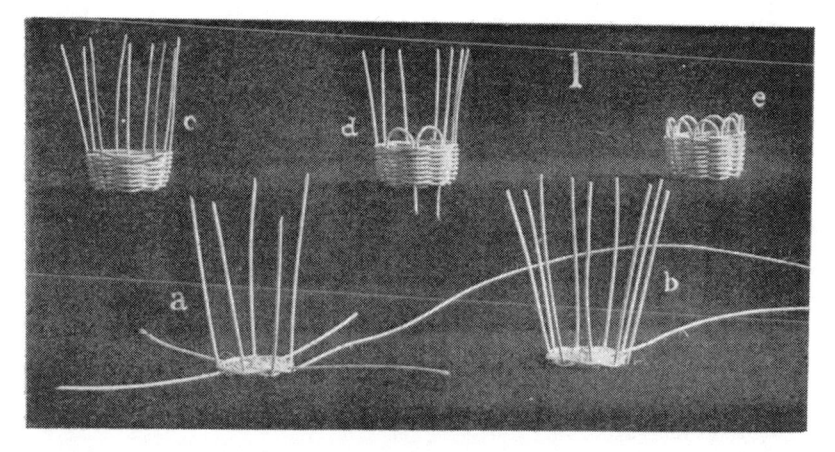

Figure 4, a, b, and c, illustrates another simple and very effective construction. The bottom is made with the pairing weave as described and illustrated in chapter II, Fig. 9. Four reeds cross four reeds, thus giving sixteen spokes. When the bottom is woven to about two inches in diameter, turn up the spokes as at a, bringing the weavers to the outside. Behind these two and beside a stake, insert a third weaver as shown at b, and weave three rows of triple weaving, chapter I, Fig. 9. Stop this weaving by pushing each weaver down behind and beside a stake and out through the bottom of the basket. Figure 4, c, shows the three weavers as they stick out below the bottom of the basket.* Commence the single weaving by the Indian method, chapter I, Fig. 4, and continue it until the desired height has been woven. Insert

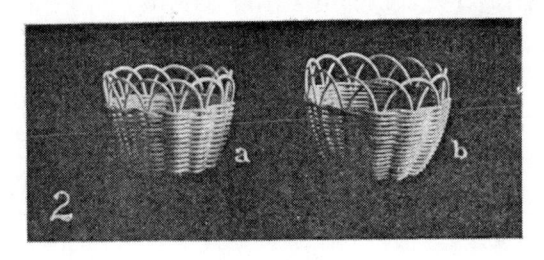

two more weavers and weave three rows of triple weaving before making the border. Notice the bands formed by this triple weaving.

The border may be closed by one or the other of the closed borders illustrated in chapter III, Fig. 2. For small baskets, c is the best closed border I have found. For baskets 5 to 7 inches in diameter b is best, and for those up to 8 or 9 inches use d.

When the single weaving is used for the main body of the basket, and bands of triple weaving are used at the top and bottom, a pleasing variety of designs may be made by weaving either the bands of colored weavers and the body of natural ones, or *vice versa*.

Figure 5 illustrates the consecutive steps in the making of the twisted handles shown in the lower row of Figure 4. The illustra-

---

*If the weaving is too tight to admit of pushing the weavers down beside the stakes, use a common scratch awl to make room for them. One cannot use the awl too freely in closing borders and making handles.

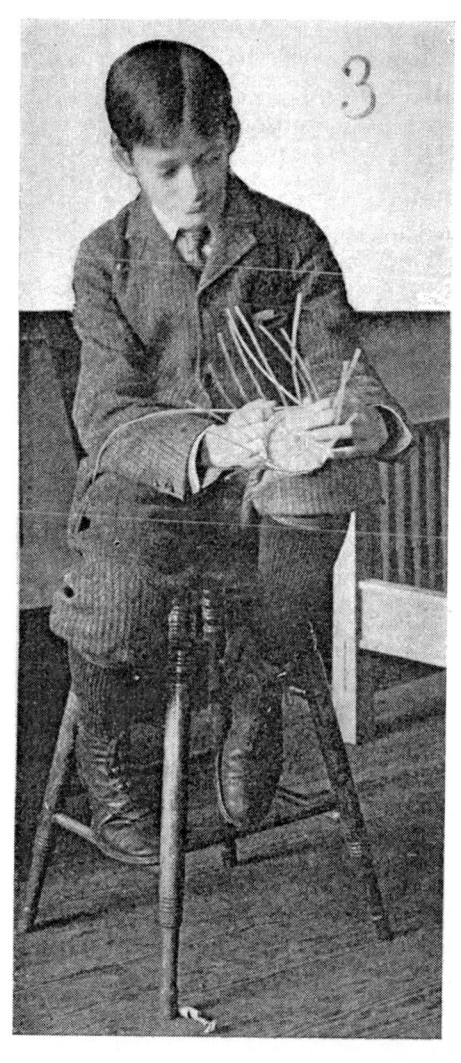

tive work is wound around a piece of wood which takes the place of the upper edge of the basket. A piece of 4 reed is inserted beside the stakes on opposite sides of the rim as shown at Figure 4e. This forms the foundation of the handles, shown on f and j. For the other baskets in Figure 4 two pieces are used. One is inserted beside a stake on one side of the basket, and the other just opposite beside another stake. These are then curved over and inserted beside the third and fourth stake from where they were first inserted, thus forming the semi-circular foundation on which the twisting is done.

A reed, wet until very pliable, is now inserted to the left of the right-hand side of the foundation reed, Fig. 5, I. This is now twisted three times around the foundation reed, and comes to the outside of the basket, as shown at 2. It is now put through to the inside of the basket, outside of the foundation reed, just below the closed border,* and brought to the front just below the first twisting, as shown at 3. Follow the first twist back to the starting point, keeping the weaver beside the first twist. Do not let the weaver cross the first one. Keep it beside the first at all times. It now goes to the inside, and is put through to the outside to the

right of the foundation reed, and brought up as at 4, and twisted to the left beside the first two until it reaches the point a, where the first, almost universal, error is made. The reed should go to the left of the one already there, as shown at 5, then to the inside of the basket and up to the front, as shown at 6. Twist it back beside the others, put it to the inside and again to the outside to the right of the second. Look out for error b at this point. Figure 7 is correct. Go back and forth once more, and finish as shown at 8. Figure 9 shows the completed handle.

*This is not absolute. It may be put through much further down if desired, say two, three, or even four rows below the border.

The secret of a good handle is in adjusting the ratio of the foundation weaver, diameter of semi-circle, and number of twists so that when the winding is completed the handle will have the appearance of a closely twisted rope. The handle just described has a 1⅜ inch semi-circular foundation of No. 4 reed, and is bound with No. 2 reed twisted three times around to start with. Winding should always continue until the foundation reed is completely covered. Figure 5, c, shows a handle with a 2 inch semi-circular foundation of No. 4 reed twisted three times around with No. 3 reed. D has a foundation of No. 5 reed twisted with No. 2 reed four twists, and e is another, adapted to a larger basket as a bail handle. Its dimensions and the number of twists are clearly shown. The foundation is No. 5 reed, and the winding weaver is of No. 3. These are sufficient to enable one to judge the ratio which will give a good handle.

In order to take advantage of the constructive decorative features spoken of in chapter I, it is necessary to know how to get the correct number of spokes for any desired diameter of bottom, as the woven figures spoken of in that article are dependent upon the ratio of the number of stakes to the number of weavers. When the bottom of a basket is less than 4 inches in diameter, it is well to have the stakes not more than ½ inch apart, and in those from 4 to 6 inches not more than ¾ inch apart.

It is also my practice in making baskets less than 3 inches in diameter to have the spokes turn up and form the stakes, and for those larger to cut spokes only long enough for the bottom, and insert one stake each side of each spoke after the bottom is woven. This gives twice as many stakes as spokes. When you find out the desired size for the bottom of the basket, decide on the number of stakes. An illustration or two will give you the method of getting this number: For instance, if nine stakes were wanted, have two long spokes cross two long spokes and insert one short spoke, as shown in chapter II. Figs. 2, 3, and 4. Weave the bottom the desired diameter, and turn up the nine spokes as stakes. If eighteen stakes were wanted, cut spokes as above only long enough for the bottom. When it is woven insert a stake each side of each spoke, and the result is eighteen stakes.

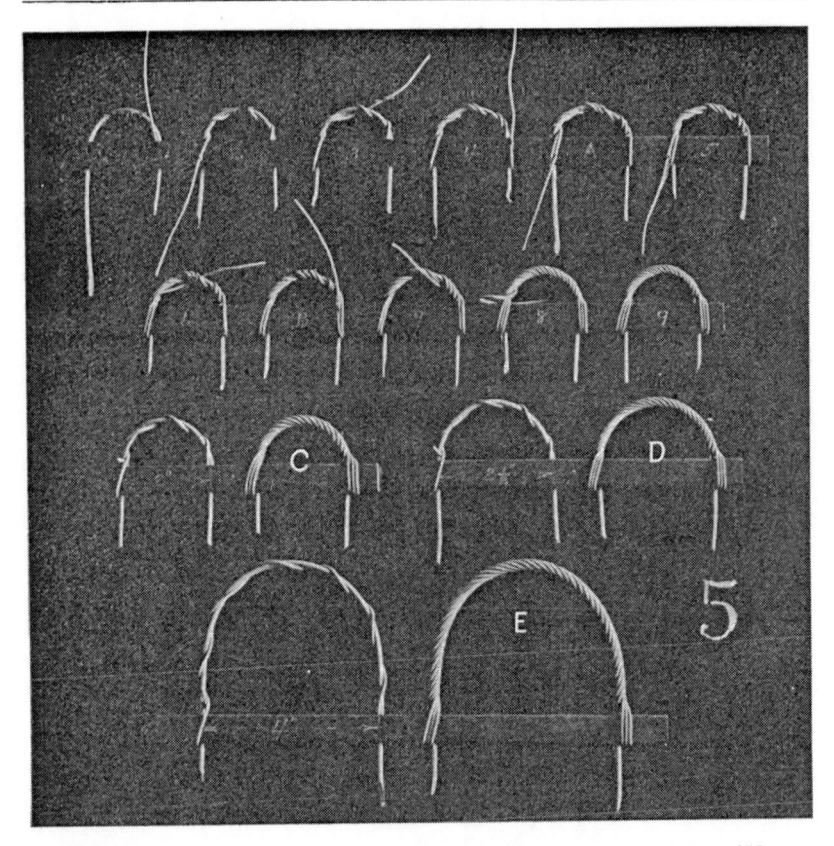

Three spokes crossing three spokes and turning up when the bottom is woven gives twelve stakes, and if the spokes are cut only long enough for the bottom and a stake inserted each side of each one the result will be twenty-four stakes.

Four crossing four and turning up will give sixteen, and by insertion thirty-two.

Five crossing five and turning up will give twenty, and by insertion forty.

Then, again, if one is not extra careful to get the spacing of the spokes equal, it will be found easy, when the bottom is partly woven, to insert a stake where two are too far apart or to cut out one where they are too near together. This will never be noticed when the bottom is fully woven. One can easily see that in this way one can get any number of stakes on which to weave. By reference to chapter I, anyone can find the ratio between stakes and weavers used in making the baskets shown in Figure 4. All are made with the triple weave and colored and natural weavers; f and j are about 1¾ inches in diameter at the bottom, g about 4 inches, and h and i about 3½ inches.

The decorative initial at the beginning of this chapter shows the adaptation of decorative weavers in making a small demijohn. Its foundation is a quart Vichy bottle. The weavers used can be easily seen, also the proportionate spacing of bands. The handles are twisted just as on a basket. Stakes and handle foundations are of No. 4 and the weavers of No. 2.

Figure 6 shows a small jug covered with weaving part way up. This was selected for its outline and covered, because it had a large "trade mark" glazed upon its surface. The baskets shown in Figure 6 will be described later.

I purposely omit detailed dimensions. They should be suggested by the one making the basket. What would seem correct to me might offend another, and I do not care to be misunderstood as wishing to force my own taste in matters of proportion upon any one else.

Be yourself fully and completely, and let your work exemplify the fact that you are doing your own thinking and simply using the information you acquire as suggestive of greater possibilities.

V. CIRCULAR BASKETS

THIS chapter deals with the construction of the basket usually called a workbasket, but it may be taken as typical of all circular baskets without handles. Figure I, A and B, shows a view looking into the basket. Notice that a portion of the weaving about the center of the bottom is done with the pairing weave, until the spokes are separated sufficiently to allow triple weaving. The

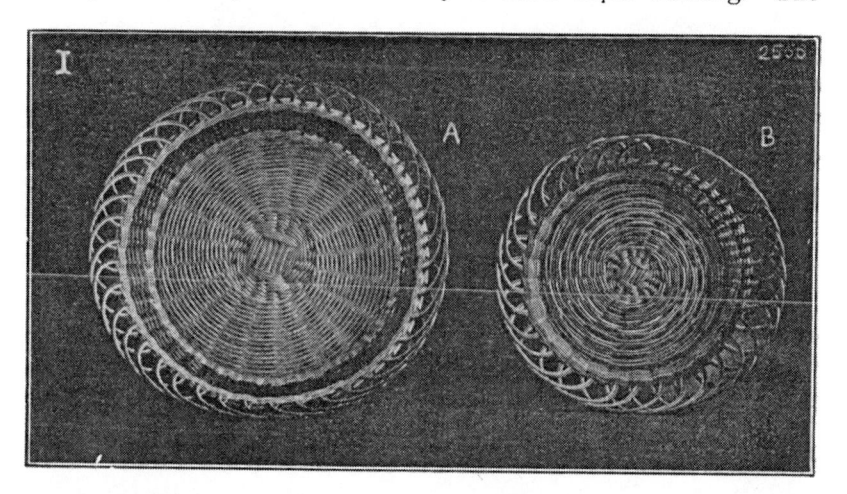

bottom is then completed with the triple weaving making it much finer in appearance. B shows the effect of using one colored weaver and two natural ones.

When the bottom is woven, cut four times as many stakes as spokes, one-half colored and one-half natural. These stakes should be about six inches longer than twice the finished height of the basket. Insert one colored and one natural, as a pair, each side of each spoke in the bottom, as shown in Figure II, A, being careful to keep the colored ones either to the right or left

41

of the natural ones. After turning up these stakes weave three rows of triple weaving, and finish this weaving by pulling the weavers through, as shown in Figure II, B. These three weavers which form the lower band of weaving may be of natural or colored

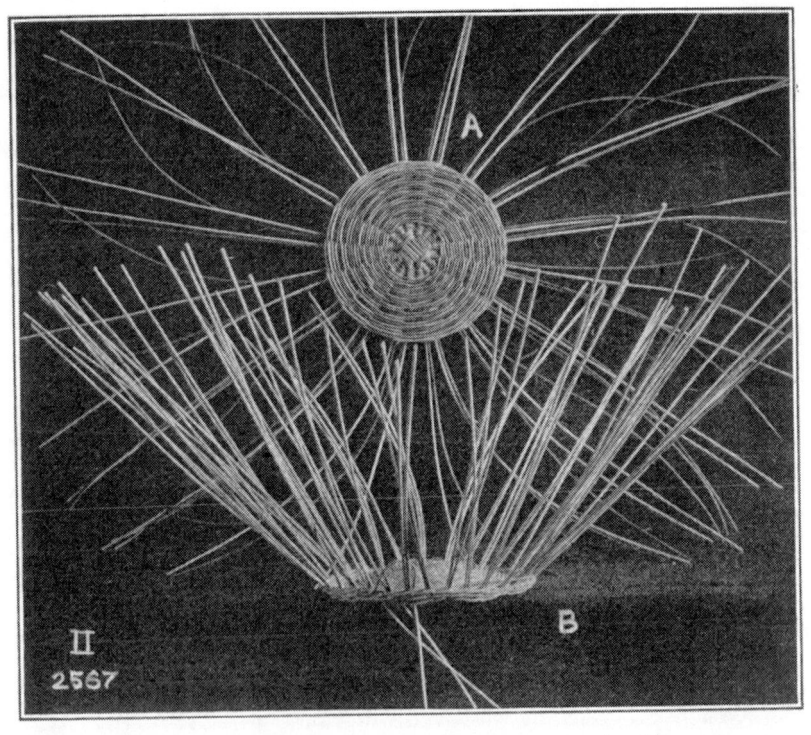

weavers. This of course depends entirely upon the ideas one has concerning the appearance of the finished basket.

Allow the stakes to flare a little more than is desired in the finished basket, as the turning over of the stakes draws the top in slightly. If an open space is wanted between the bands of triple weaving, weave one or two rows of flat weavers before weaving the second row of triple weavers, as shown in Figure III, A. This

Figure III, 2568

Figure IV, 2569

may be cut out after the basket is completed if one desires to insert a ribbon. Figure III, B, shows a basket just before the stakes are turned and with the space between the two rows of triple weaving filled up with single weaving. Figure IV, A and B, shows the method of turning over the stakes. The ends are inserted through the outer loops of the triple weave three and one-half spaces to the right or left of where the stake itself comes through the upper row of triple weaving. By turning to the right or left the colored weaver may be brought outside, regardless of how it

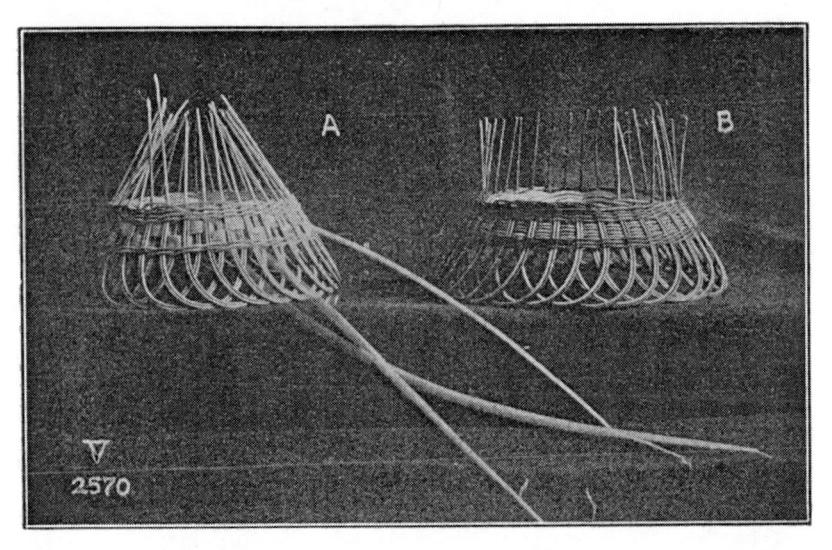

may be inserted in the bottom. When the colored bands are used it is well to have the outer stake of the colored, as at B. The tucking in of the stakes is now continued until all completed when the basket is turned bottom side up and the loops all made to touch a flat surface. Great care must be taken in doing this, as the finished appearance of the basket may be greatly marred by lack of attention to this particular point.

At this point decide whether the bottom rows of weaving are to be colored or natural; if colored, cut away the natural weavers at the bottom of the basket, as shown at Figure V, A. Next insert three weavers and weave one row of triple weaving in order that the remaining stakes may be brought to an upright position, as shown at Figure V, B. The bottom of the basket is now ready to close in. Take one upright stake, pass it in front of two, and to the inside and let it lay along the inside edge of the bottom; take each successive stake and do the same thing, as shown at Figure V, B. Figure VI, A, shows the appearance of the ends of

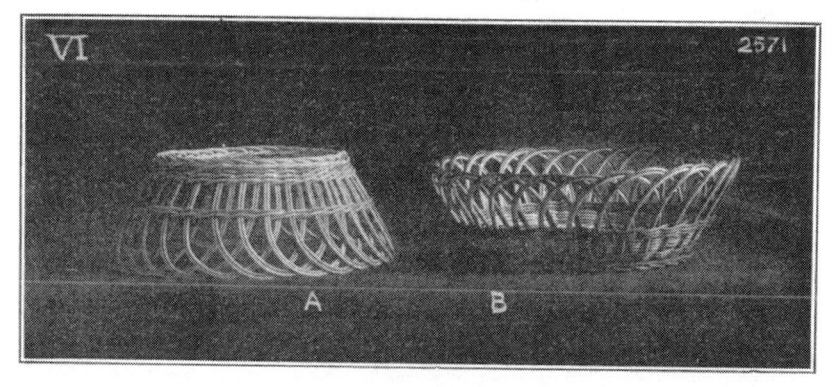

these stakes as they lay along the inside edge of the bottom. This view also shows the space which may be used for the insertion of ribbon, after cutting out the filling of flat weavers. Figure VI, B, shows the appearance of the basket when completed with the single weaving as a filler between the two rows of triple weaving.

The basket illustrated in Figure VI, chapter 4, was made by this process; it was eight inches in diameter at the bottom and had a twenty spoke center.

The basket illustrated in Figure I, B, of this chapter has a sixteen spoke center and a bottom five and one-half inches in diameter. The height of the loops in baskets of this kind is something that each worker must settle for himself. The tendency at first will be to get them too high. The combinations of color and proportion which may be worked out in baskets of this description are innumerable. I know of no construction which requires more artistic taste and a finer sense of correct proportion.

VI. ELLIPTICAL BASKETS

WHEN one has attained a certain degree of proficiency in making round baskets it is but natural that he should desire to make those which are elliptical in shape. The making of these baskets presents a problem which has been difficult to solve and the solution of which renders their construction practical for school uses. In a circular basket, where an even tension is kept on the weaver during the weaving process, the sides come up with an even flare but the stakes have a tendency to lean. This is due to the constant tension from left to right and works havoc in the construction of elliptical baskets. Unless great care is taken the upper edge of the basket will be shaped like the unfinished one illustrated in Figure II.

This tendency troubled me for a long time until I noticed that this warping commenced in the weaving of the bottoms and increased as the sides of the basket were woven. If the bottoms are woven left-handed or bottom side up, without regard to this warping, and then, after the stakes are inserted, the weaving of the sides proceeds as usual, but little care need be exercised in order to get an even basket as shown in Figure II. The warping tendency produced by weaving the sides offsets that produced by the left-handed weaving of the bottoms.

Since the discovery of this little trick the weaving of elliptical baskets has been a constant pleasure and has been carried on with marked success.

Figure I represents the consecutive steps in the construction of elliptical bottoms. Cut four spokes of No. 4 or No. 5 reed the length of the major diameter of the bottom, and as many as are desired, the length of the minor diameter. By analysis it will be seen that these bottoms are half round at each end and filled in straight between; therefore, each end requires half as many spokes as would be required in a round bottom, and as many in between these as is necessary in order to get the bottom the required length.

Another important point,—if the spokes on each end are to

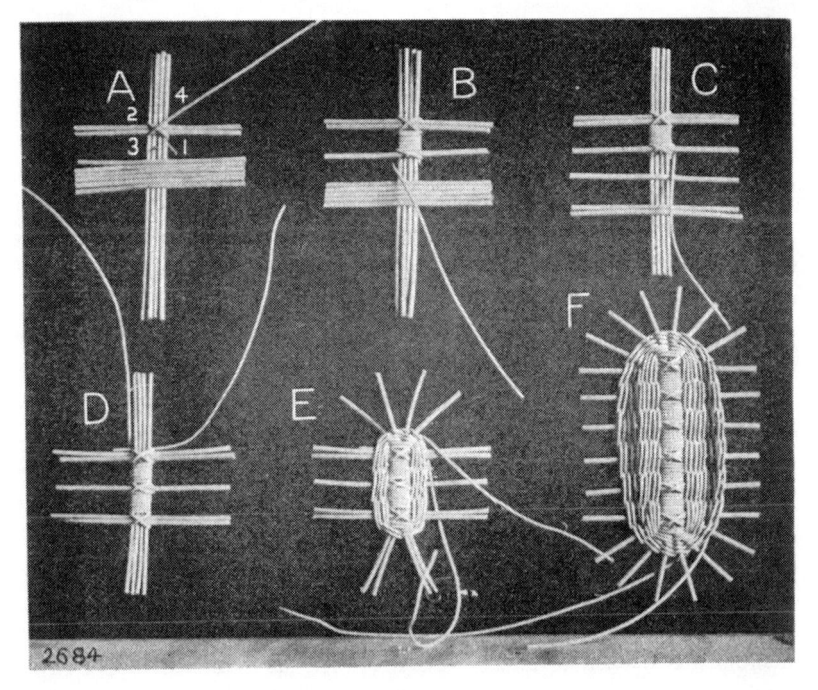

Figure I.

be one inch apart when the bottom is all woven, the spokes between must be a little more than that distance apart as these side spokes remain parallel during the weaving of the sides while the end ones radiate somewhat with the flare of the basket. Split all the short spokes and string them on the four long ones. Take a pair of the short spokes and put them near the end of the long ones as shown at A, Fig. I. Place a weaver of No. 2 or No. 3 reed, diagonally behind the group from 1 to 2 and bring it diagonally across the front from 2 to 1, then back of the group of four and to the left from 1 to 3, parallel with the short pair of spokes. Next, diagonally across the face from 3 to 4 and down behind the short pair from 4 to 1. Now the winding of the four long spokes commences as

Figure II.

shown. This should continue for about $1\frac{3}{16}$ inches, if the end spokes are to be one inch apart when the bottom is finished.

Bring in the next spoke and bind it into its place. This binding is so clearly shown as to require no explanation. When all the short single spokes are bound in, bind in the last pair as shown, turn the bottom and insert the second weaver in order that the pairing weave may be started. D, Fig. I, shows just how this weave is inserted.

The weaving process from now on is just the same as for that of round bottoms described in the chapter on Weaving Foundations. E, Fig. I, shows the proper relative position of the spokes at the beginning of the separation of the end ones into singles.

If it is thought more desirable to have the sides of the bottom a little curved rather than straight, the straight part may be filled in after all the spokes are separated into singles. This is illustrated, and is done with the colored weavers in order to show it more clearly. This filling in process is done with the single weave, over and

Figure III.

under five spokes for the first two pieces, then three, two and one. If this does not round the sides to suit the taste fill in again after one or two rows of regular weaving.

When the bottom is woven, insert one stake each side of each spoke and weave the sides as in the usual way. One can easily figure out the proper number of stakes required, in order to take advantage of the decorative features of triple weaving, in these baskets as in the round ones. Figure III shows some elliptical baskets of different designs and proportions as to major and minor diameters and also two kinds of twisted handles, small and large. Basket No. 3 has a bottom with but one single spoke between its ends as shown in Figure I, D and E. Basket No. 2 has two as shown at C. Basket No. 1 has three, and No. 4 and No. 5 have six.

The edge finishes are all as described in chapter III, Fig. II, B, and the twisted handles are all as described in chapter IV. A pleasing decorative feature is shown in the large wastebasket in the left hand foreground of Figure III. Two natural and one colored weaver are used and the stakes are equally divisible by three, the number of weavers. Three rows are woven around, then the green weaver changes places with a white one and three more rows are woven. This process is kept up until the desired height is reached, resulting in a spiral arrangement of spots. Figure III shows progress in working out some simple designs, A showing a large hollow diamond (as easily made solid). Smaller hollow diamonds would look well around an elliptical basket. B also shows hollow diamonds and the Indian "good luck" symbol. This work is done with the single weave on stakes not more than one-half inch apart.

Many fine designs may be "worked up" on plotting paper. Use paper which is lined off about as far apart as the diameter of the weaver to be used and draw vertical lines across this about as far apart as the distance between the stakes.

TURNER   THE BASKET MAKER

VII. MELON SHAPED BASKETS

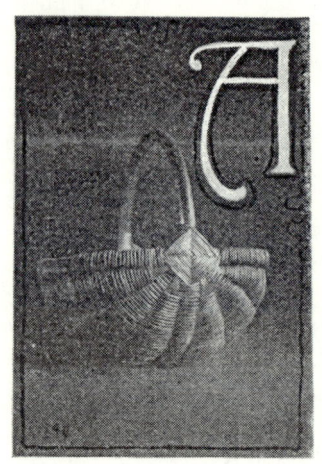

A MELON shaped basket seems to me to be the most fascinating of all in its method of construction. Figure I shows the material necessary with the exception of the weavers. Figure II shows the method of determining the shape of the slices or ribs on which the weaving is done.* The material with which the two circular ribs are made is stout ash splint. Take two straight pieces the length required for the circumference of the circle allowing about three-fourths of an inch for lap. These may be fastened together to form the two circular rings either by a small bent iron fastener or with fine string. These rings are then placed in the position shown in Figure III, No. 1, perpendicular to each other. The weaver is then placed behind the vertical

*NOTE.—Let AA represent the orthographic projection of the two rings. From the point x, with a radius equal to xy, draw the quarter circle. Divide this quarter circle into three equal parts from 1 to y, and connect the points of division with lines to point x. Lay off lines parallel to these one-eighth inch apart to represent the space to be allowed for the weavers. This will show the projection of one side of the basket with the ribs in position. Draw a quarter circle on the right hand side. From the center line, at point 2, lay off distances on this quadrant about an inch apart as shown at 2-a-b-c-d. Project these to the left on to the line xy, and with x as a center, continue these projection lines with arcs crossing the center rib, as shown. Draw chords 4, 5, 6, 7, and 8. Take a piece of stiff paper or of the material to be used as ribs and bend around from 1 to 3 to get the true length which will be the distance 1 2 3 as shown above at B. Draw the two center lines at right angles, crossing at 4. Lay off distances 4 5, 5 6, 6 7, 7 8 on either side of 4 corresponding with the distances 2a, ab, bc, and cd. On these, by means of arcs, lay off distances equal to the lengths of the corresponding chords 4, 5, 6, 7, and 8 in the view AA. A curve tangent to these arcs shows one contour of a rib.

If many baskets of this size are wanted it will be found convenient to make a pattern for each size and mark it properly. If the basket wanted is more than six inches in diameter more ribs will be needed, and the small lay-out C will give the proper suggestion.

52

ring on top of the horizontal ring with its ends projecting toward the right in the direction of A-B. The weaver is then brought over from A to D in front of the vertical ring.

Then behind the horizontal ring and up to B, in which position it is shown at No. 1. From thence it goes diagonally across the vertical ring from B to C and upward behind the horizontal, from

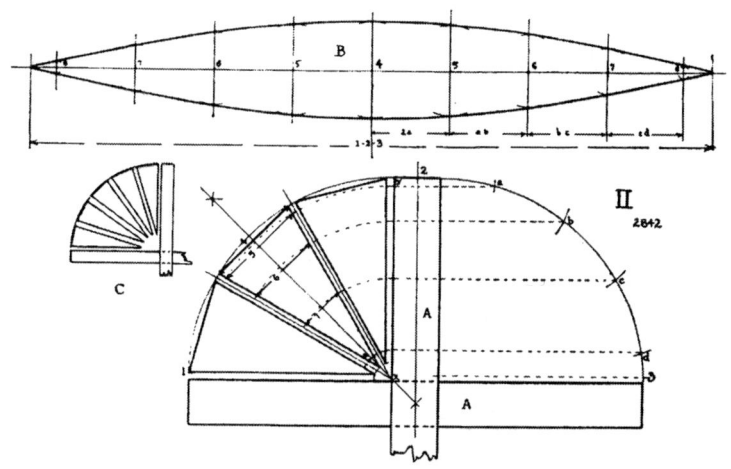

C to A and assumes the position shown at No. 2. It now goes across from A to D as before, and behind the vertical ring from D to C, below the horizontal; which position is shown at No. 3. From there it goes across the vertical ring from C to B, then behind the vertical from B to A. This method of winding is kept up, as shown at 4, 5, and 6, until a little pocket is formed, as shown at E and F. This process takes place on both ends of the rings. The center ribs on either side are now put into this pocket and the single weaving is commenced, as shown at Figure IV.

Weave three or four rows on one end, then three or four on the other end. This weaving, first on one end and then on the

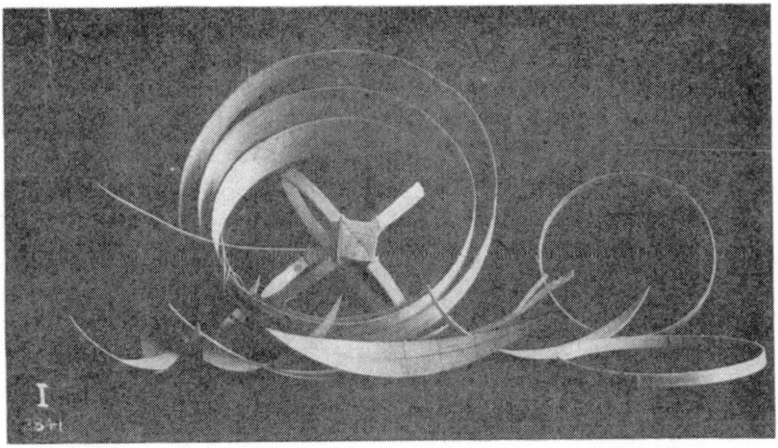
I

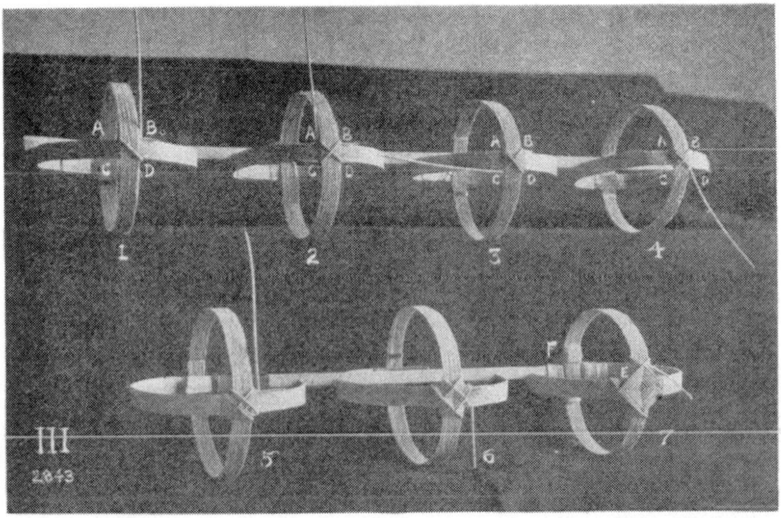
A
B
C
D
1
2
3
4
5
6
7
F
E
III

other, must be kept up during the whole construction of the basket.

In the construction of these baskets many will place all the ribs in the pocket at once, but this method of construction is too difficult for an amateur to attempt.

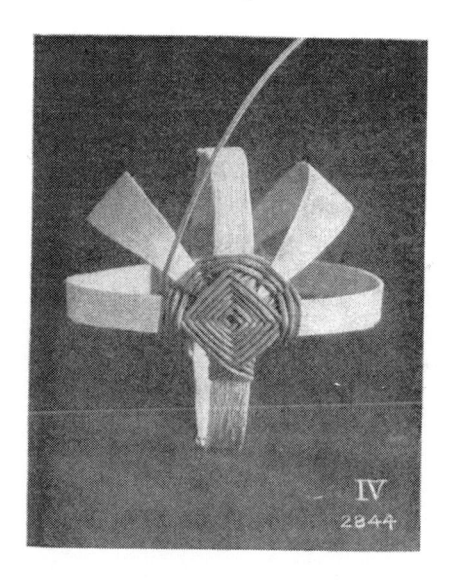

IV
2844

After these two middle ribs have been placed in position and three rows of weaving completed, the other four ribs should be tucked into the pocket on one end and the single weaving continued until four or five rows are woven, as shown in Figure V.

This process has been found to be much easier than to place the ribs in both pockets, because of the fact that in weaving on one end the other ends of the ribs are continually flying out.

After four or five rows are woven the other ends of the ribs may be placed in the opposite pocket and the weaving continued as on the opposite end. Great care must be taken in the shaping of these ribs to see that there is a proper distance between them so that the weaver may not be cramped.

The final shape of the basket depends almost entirely upon the nicety with which these ribs are constructed.

If one wishes to construct the basket so that it will be more than a half-sphere in depth, it can be easily done by making a plan of rings and ribs of the shape wanted and laying out these rings and ribs from that. It may be necessary in teaching younger pupils the construction of these baskets for the teacher to do the drawing and laying out of the size and shape of these ribs, but this process should be thoroughly explained.

If difficulty is found in getting heavy ash splint for the rings and ribs, they may be easily constructed from the hoops of a sugar barrel or even wood from a cheese box, both of which must be soaked and whittled down thin, say to one-sixteenth of an inch in thickness. One of the best melon shaped baskets which I have seen had its rings and ribs constructed from wood taken from a butter box which was about eight inches in diameter. Too much emphasis cannot be placed on the necessity of getting the foundation features of this construction absolutely accurate. This is truer of this shape than of almost any other.

Where it seems impossible to get either the ash splint or other material spoken of, No. 8 or 10 round reed may be split lengthwise and used in the construction of the rings. If these are to be used it will be found necessary to have a greater number of ribs on which to weave than has been spoken of previously. It does not seem wise, however, to attempt a melon shaped basket over four or five inches in diameter with half round reed as a foundation.

"Think it up a little" and see how broad the field of basketry really may become.

CPSIA information can be obtained
at www.ICGtesting.com
Printed in the USA
LVOW12s1125271216
518822LV00004B/247/P